POPULAR MUSIC HARMONY

VOLUME II

JEFF GARDNER

CADENCES AND HARMONIC SEQUENCES

Copyright @ 2016 by Jeff Gardner.

Copyright @ 2016 by Jeff Gardner
All rights reserved. No part of this book may be used or reproduced without the express written consent of the author.

First Edition

Music Engraving:
Jeff Gardner

Graphic design:
Leo Viana

Cover painting:
Lisa Gardner

Back cover photo:
Fernando Natalici

TABLE OF CONTENTS

IIm7 V7/ IMaj7 Cadences	15
IIm7 V7/ IMaj7 Cadences Descending by Whole Steps	21
IIm7 V7sus4/ IMaj7 Cadences	24
II V/ I Cadences with Rhythmic Feels	25
II V/ I Cadences in Drop 2	31
IIm7b5 V7/ Im7 Cadences	33
bVI7 V7/ Im7 Cadences	35
IIm7 bII7/ Im7 Cadences	36
IIm7 bIIMaj7/ Imaj7 & IIm7 bII7/ Imaj7 Cadences	37
IIm7b5 V7/ Im7 Cadences with Rhythmic Feels	38
IIm7 V7/ Im7 Cadences	40
IIm7 V7/ IMaj7 Melodic Cadences	42
Melodic Line on the Harmony of "Tune Up"	46
Approach Tones	47
Melodic Line on the Harmony of "Solar"	53
Loops Based on the Cycle of Fifths	54
II IV/ I Cadences	57
Cadences with Delayed Resolution	58
Minor Key Melodic II IV/ I Cadences	59
Melodic Line on the Harmony of "Beautiful Love"	61
Melodic Line on the Harmony of "How High the Moon"	63
Cadences with a Dominant Seventh Tonic	66
Melodic Cadences with Dominant Seventh Tonic	68
Melodic Line on the Harmony of "Laura"	70
Melodic Line on the Harmony of "A Foggy Day"	72
Deceptive Cadences	75
Deceptive Cadences with Resolution	76
Chord Changes for "Barquinho"	77
Countermelody for "Barquinho"	78
II bII/ I Cadences	80
Cadences with Phrygian Dominant	81
Gospel and Plagai Cadences	82
Bitonal Cadences	84
Cadences with Maj7#5 "Slash" chords on V	85
Harmonic Sequences with Major Seventh Tonic	86
Harmonic Sequences with Dominant Seventh Tonic	87
Harmonic Sequences with Minor Seventh Tonic	91
Harmonic Sequences Starting on II	95
Harmonic Sequences with 7sus4 Tonic	96
Harmonic Sequences Starting on III	97
Coltrane Changes	98
Modulating Harmonic Sequences	99
Modulating Melodic Harmonic Sequences	100
Melodic Line on the Harmony of "My One and Only Love"	104
Melodic Harmonic Sequences - Im7 VI7/ IIm7b5 V7	106
Melodic Harmonic Sequences Starting on III	108
Melodic Line on the Harmony of "Giant Steps"	110
Mixed Harmonic Sequences	113
Rhythm Changes	117
Melodic Line on the Harmony of de Rhythm Changes	119
Melodic Line on the Harmony of "All of Me"	121
Reharmonization of "All of Me"	123
Harmonic Sequences with Pedal Points	124
"Some Day My Prince Will Come" with Pedal Point	127
Double Pedal Points	128
Composition Exercises with Cadences and Harmonic Sequences	129
Music for Analysis	130

DEDICATION

To my teachers - Ruth Schontal, Nadia Boulanger, Ivan Tcherepnin, Jaki Byard, Don Friedman, Chucho Valdes, John Lewis, Hall Overton, and Charles Banacos – my deep gratitude

To my family - Rosa, Gabriela, Maiara, Lisa, and Leila – eternal love

To my graphic designer Leo Viana for his brilliant work and his patience

To my friends - Rubner Abreu, Paulo Levi, Bruno Py, Alciomar Oliveira, Thiago Marques, Waldenir Duarte, Robenare Marques, Paul de Castro, Tony Dagradi, Steve Masakovski, Mike Pellera, Mike Holober, Rick Condit, Cornelius Claudio Kreusch, Dr. Michael Hittman, Ian Guest, Dr. Jacques Boucher, Carlo Sacchi, Petra Schatz, Ania Paz, Henry Jeria, Elaine Rosner, Charles Hardy, Ross Zucker, Jur and Nisha Strobos, Dr. Benjamin Gilbert, and all the great musicians I have shared the stage and the road with and from whom I have learned so much on this endless musical journey.

PREFACE

One does not compose music with theory, said Debussy. Stravinsky said that "theory does not exist" - and continues, paradoxically, "composing involves a deep intuition for theory".

One thing is certain - the relation between theory and practice occupies an important place in the reflections and writings of composers and music scholars, but, all speculation aside, reality presents itself in simple terms - theory is born from practice.

If we trust common sense, theory and practice are antagonistic ideas. It is often affirmed that theory is that which does not work in practice, but one might clarify that this is bad theory, and that good theory is that which, in essence, organizes a practice. It could not be otherwise. In music, tonal and harmonic syntax were also born from practice that was later studied and organized.

Historically, the underlying concepts of tonal harmony are the consequence of a long process. In Ancient Greece, Pythagoras formulated the concepts of consonance and dissonance. However, for Pythagoras, consonances were simple mathematical relationships and dissonances were complex mathematical relationships. Thus formulated, major seconds, being simple mathematical relationships, were consonances, and major thirds, being complex mathematical relationships, were considered dissonances. Only long afterwards, at the end of the Middle Ages, in the fourteenth century, musicians began to replace Pythagorian theory with actual perception of audio phenomena, and major and minor thirds came to be perceived as imperfect consonances. This conceptual change replaced the mathematical basis with a physiological and empirical base. What was now important was that, in reality, we perceive and react to the phenomenon of simultaneity, and out of this grew a fundamental structural principle: dissonances must resolve to consonances, tensions move toward resolutions. Also in the fourteenth century, the first cadences using the leading tone appeared, the seventh degree a half step below the tonic. These changes made way for two essential ideas that appeared later: the concept of chords and that of tonality.

The idea of a chord appeared in the Renaissance. Gioseffo Zarlino, in his treatise Instutioni harmoniche (1558), speaks of two types of perfect chords - major and minor. He also attributes to the bass the role of sustaining the harmonic structure. In this sense, it is worth noting that, for Zarlino, the chord is not a harmonic entity, but an agreement, having as its basis perfect and imperfect consonances. Therefore, the chord in the polyphonic music of the sixteenth century is mainly the result of the superposition of melodic lines. The concept of a chord, as we know it today, began in 1612, when Johannes Lippius, recognized the inversions and established the difference between the bass and the root. But it is during the seventeenth century that the bases of harmony and of the tonal system are established and the ancient modes begin to disappear, to be replaced by the system based on transpositions of the Ionian and Aeolian modes. Instrumental improvisation is widely used concomitant with a type of simplified notation called figured bass. This period is characterized by an intense practice, during which time there are no practical treatises, but rather manuals teaching the practice of basso continuo, a process analogous to walking bass and also its predecessor. And it is during this same period that modulation and its procedures are established as part of the creative and structural process. The great composer of this period, Claudio Monteverdi, calls the process based on the melody-chord relationship seconda pratica, in contrast with prima pratica, based on counterpoint and polyphonic procedures. And, after more than a century of much practice and little theory, in 1722 there appeared the Traité de l'Harmonie, by the French composer Jean-Philippe Rameau. This was in effect the first theoretical postulate on harmony. Rameau underscored the importance of the cycle of fifths and of the relationships between the roots of chords. In the nineteenth century, Simon Sechter reorganized and deepened Rameau's theory. The ideas of Sechter and Rameau formed the basis of two of the most important treatises of the twentieth century - Theory of Harmony, by Schoenberg, and Harmony, de Walter Piston; the latter being, perhaps, the principal theoretical basis for the majority of books on Jazz harmony published up until today.

Another major advance in the comprehension of the harmonic phenomenon occurred around 1884, with the formulation of the theory of functions, by the German professor and theoretician Hugo Riemann. Riemann's theory can be summed up in the central idea that - in the major and minor scales there are seven chords, and therefore, seven degrees, but only three functions - tonic, subdominant, and dominant. Riemann established a basic difference between degree and function: the former is a topological concept referring to the position of the chord in the scale; function, in turn, occurs in the phrase and refers to the sensation that a given chord creates in its relation with others. Curiously, it is only now in the twenty first century that Rameau's theory of the relationships between roots and the theory of functions created by Riemann, are being perceived as part of a historical process, and their complementarity is being appreciated and understood. Here in Brasil, Ian Guest, in his book Harmony, a Practical Method, published in 2006, integrates in a practical and objective fashion these two approaches.

The present work, Popular Music Harmony, by composer-pianist Jeff Gardner, expands on ideas presented in his Jazz Piano: Creative Concepts and Techniques, published in France in 1997, a book in which Jeff laid out his vision of the processes and techniques that shape his practice. The present project derives from the very bases of the harmonic system since its origin: cycles, cadences, and sequences. It is important to point out that the concepts contained in the three volumes of Popular Music Harmony were born out of a daily practice of creation and improvisation. This approach opens up the thought processes of the student used to thinking about the structure of isolated chords, forcing him or her to engage in a more chromatic way of thinking. The perfect fifth (together with its inversion, the perfect fourth) is the only interval that generates a complete cycle of 12 notes. The semitone - the other interval that generates the chromatic spectrum - does not generate cycles but rather chromatic steps. For this reason, volumes I and II of Popular Music Harmony offer piano students and other instrumentalists a program of essential exercises based on the backbone of the tonal system: transpositions of cycles, cadences, and harmonic sequences.

Rubner de Abreu

CADENCES AND HARMONIC SEQUENCES

The cycle of fourths/fifths is omnipresent in many styles of music. The root movement of perfect fourth ascending or perfect fifth descending may suggest a dominant-tonic relationship in many situations. However, the cycle alone does not establish a tonic or tonal center. It is best thought of as the smoothest and most traditional way of getting "from point A to point B" harmonically. Many cadences contain a fragment of the cycle of fourths/fifth, however they are different because they have a beginning, middle, and end, this last chord being usually but not always the tonic. An erroneous idea has been spread through the indiscriminate use of the term "II V", frequently applied to any root movement of perfect fourth ascending or perfect fifth descending with a minor seventh chord moving to a dominant seventh chord. It seems quite obvious that where a tonal center is not established, it is incorrect to designate a chord as "II" or "V" without a tonal context. For example, this series of chords:

Dm7 G7/ Bm7 E7/ Abm7 Db7/ F#m7 B7

cannot be analyzed in relation to a tonic. The root movements of perfect fourth ascending or perfect fifth descending are no more than that. They can be conceived as fragments of the cycle of fourths/fifths but it is senseless to call them "II V"s. This becomes all the more evident when we change the chord qualities, for example:

DMaj7 G7sus4/ BMaj7 E7sus4/ AbMaj7 Db7sus4/ F#Maj7 B7sus4

Let us have the courage to conceive compositions or sections thereof as lacking a tonic, without being atonal, instead of forcing our analysis to conform to seventeenth or eighteenth century music theory.

Cadences and harmonic sequences, together with the cycle of fourths/fifths, form the basis for a large share of the harmony of modern popular music. A cadence is a series of chords, traditionally drawn from the diatonic chords of a key, which establishes a tonic or tonal center. In modern music these diatonic chord qualities are often modified and their roots may also be substituted. In a wider context, the notion of tonality has expanded to include many chords used as a tonic which are not traditionally considered as possible tonic chords, such as Maj7#5, diminished sevenths, sus4, 7sus4b9, and slash chords, also called triads with non-diatonic bass tones (please see Some Thoughts on Tonality for an in-depth discussion of this idea). The dominant seventh chord is the tonic of the majority of compositions in blues, rock, funk, and R & B as well as many compositions in the jazz idiom, often with a tonal color defined by the blues scale – with both major and minor thirds, thus placing much of these musical styles firmly outside the traditionally separate major and minor tonalities of classical music theory, in which the dominant seventh chord is either on V or used as a secondary dominant, but never as a tonic. These tonic chords lend new life to traditional root movements such as II V/ I. Each mode may also determine a tonic, with or without a cadence.

The basic types of cadences – perfect, imperfect, plagal and deceptive, are used in classical music harmony as well as in modern popular music, although they are often present with different voicings. A perfect cadence ends on the tonic chord in root position. Imperfect cadences end on the tonic chord in inversion. The deceptive cadence ends on a chord other than the tonic, most often with the root of the tonic chord in the melody. A plagal cadence ends on the tonic, usually preceded by a IV or IVm chord or a IIm chord. This cadence is widely used in gospel music.

The II V/ I cadence, with its myriad possible chord qualities, is the most widely used perfect cadence, however we can also use II IV/ I and other less common root movements. Since the II V/ I has such a strong root movement, it can be extensively modified and we can still hear a tonic, often with a duration on I which is twice that of II and V. This doubled rhythmic value on the tonic helps distinguish a cadence from root movements through the cycle of fourths/fifths.

A harmonic sequence differs from a cadence in that it is often repeated. It is used not only as a compositional element within the form of a piece, but also as an introduction, extended coda ("tag"), or interlude of determinate or indeterminate duration. The most commonly used harmonic sequence - I VI/ II V, contains the II V/ I cadence if we consider that, when repeated, the last two chords resolve to the first (tonic). This sequence can be conceived as one fourth of the cycle of fifths since all four chords are adjacent in the cycle. For example, if we look at a circular chart of the twelve keys with C at the top, these four roots correspond to 9:00, 10:00, 11:00, and 12:00 on the face of a clock. I Got Rhythm is the classic example of I VI / I V in the jazz repertoire.

As is the case with cadences, harmonic sequences may or may not be derived from a specific tonality. Many sequences have modified chord qualities on one or more degrees, sometimes referred to as "modal borrowing" or "modal mixture". For instance - the diatonic sequence CMaj7 Am7 / Dm7 G7 can become CMaj7 A7 / Dmi7 G7 or CMaj7 A7 / D7 G7. Harmonic sequences do not necessarily determine a tonal center, and some may use chords from various keys. Any series of chords can be repeated, establishing a sequence without a tonic. For example:

[: Dm7 G7/ Cmi7 F7 :]

does not establish a tonal center and can be used independently, although it could theoretically be used in a tonal context by adding a resolution to BbMaj7 – producing a longer cadence – IIIm7 VI7/ IIm7 V7/ I. A harmonic sequence can also be more abstract, not even hinting at a tonal center. For example, the beginning of the solo section of my composition, "Saudade do Samurai" (each chord lasts four measures and each 16-bar sequence modulates upwards by whole steps). This ascending movement by whole steps avoids defining a single tonal area:

Dm7 / / / / Bb7 / / / / Ebm7 / / / / C7sus4 / / / /

Em7 / / / / C7 / / / / Fm7 / / / / D7sus4 / / / /   etc.

Traditional harmonic sequences, such as I VI/ II V or II V/ I VI, can be placed over a dominant pedal point, creating tension which may or may not release to the tonic of the pedal tone a perfect fourth above the pedal tone (see the Miles Davis arrangement of "Someday My Prince Will Come"). On Miles' recording of this tune, the dominant pedal is played by the bass throughout the entire first theme, resolving to the tonic chord in the first measure of the first solo chorus.

Harmonic sequences as well as cadences can move through different intervallic series. They may ascend or descend by whole or half steps, major or minor thirds, or follow the half tone-whole tone scale or augmented scale, creating a fresh perspective on traditional harmonic materials. These scales can in turn generate new harmonic sequences by placing a chord of the same quality on each note of the scale, for instance: G7sus4 / Bb7sus4 / B7sus4 / D7sus4 / Eb7sus4 / Gb7sus4 (a sequence based on the G augmented scale, from my composition Conversa Fiada).

John Coltrane introduced an important group of harmonic sequences mixing root movement intervals, thereby greatly expanding the vocabulary of harmonic structures for composition and improvisation. These sequences, used in tunes such as Giant Steps, Countdown, 26-2, Satellite, and in reharmonizations of standard tunes such as Body and Soul, have become known as "Coltrane Changes". I call these hybrid sequences, as they often alternate movements by half steps or thirds with movements in perfect fourths. Lines on these sequences are sometimes called "chord on chord", as they allow us to suggest many different harmonies over a single chord within the melodic line, thus creating tension and release. These chords may or may not be played by the harmonic instruments in the ensemble.

With increasing numbers of composers using computers to create and notate music, the concept of "loops" – repeated sections of a piece, has become relevant as applied to harmonic sequences. We can "loop" any series of chords, modifying the harmonic rhythm (the speed at which the chords change) and/or modulating, if desired. Any element may be repeated – either for an indeterminate duration (for solos, for instance) or for a pre-determined number of bars. These repeated elements, also called "vamps", may be rhythmic, melodic and/or harmonic, or any combination of these three elements. An interesting extension of this idea is what I call "interlocking loops". This term may refer to sections of a piece or repeated harmonic sequences within larger repeated sections. The following example is built from two 2-bar repeated sections that together create an 8-bar total form:

[: Dm7 G7/ Dm7 G7 :] [: Cm7 F7/ Cm7 F7 :].

The repeat, or second ending, of the loop may contain a variation of the harmony, ensuring both continuity and variety. As in each individual loop, these interlocking loops may or may not be repeated an indeterminate number of times. These interlocking loops may contain variations of the first sequence. In the following example, two sequences of two bars each are linked to form a 4-bar loop:

[: Dm7 G7/ Cm7 A7/ Dmi7 G7/Em7b5 A7 :]

The following is an example of a harmonic sequence made up of interlocking 2-bar loops, modified every fourth time to prepare a modulation – creating a series of 8 bar sections modulating up by half steps.

[: Cm7 A7/ Dm7b5 G7 :] (3X)

Cm7 A7/ Ebm7b5 Ab7/

[: Dbm7 Bb7/ Ebm7 Ab7 :] (3X)

Dbm7 Bb7/ Em7 A7/ etc.

The cadences and sequences in this book are presented in various forms: in block chords, with rhythms in styles such as jazz, samba, salsa (Afro-Cuban), and baião, as well as melodic lines. The same elements are also presented in a freer and more intuitive form in melodic lines based on standard tunes, each illustrating one or more concepts presented here. In order to assimilate this material faster, more permanently, and in a creative and enjoyable fashion, each musician or student (we are all eternal students of music!) should write lines on each concept, compose pieces and/or etudes on each idea or group of ideas, and practice improvising on each cadence or sequence, alone and in a group context. The examples in this book are written in a single key, and should be transposed in a rigorously symmetrical manner, playing each exercise with exactly the same intervals and chord voicings in every key. By so doing, the student will develop a series of reflexes enabling him or her to solo and/or accompany (in the case of harmonic instruments) compositions containing these elements. Mastering these examples in 12 keys will prepare you for sight-reading and dealing with a huge portion of the standard repertoire of many styles of music. For musicians or music students who do not consider themselves composers, writing your own exercises, studies and pieces following the models based on these structures can be a fun and effective way to develop this fundamental aspect of music. Examples of compositional strategies may be found at the end of this book.

Although this book is written on a piano staff with G and F clefs together, it is not only for pianists. The melodic lines and phrases on cadences and sequences may be played on any melodic instrument, adjusting the range where necessary. The block chords may be transformed into melodic phrases by playing them as arpeggios, using techniques such as permutation and inversion, as well as introducing alterations (the fifth may be substituted by 11, #11, 13, or b13, for example). This said, brass, string, and reed players, guitarists, bassists, and yes, drummers, have much to gain from a study of this material as chords on the piano or keyboard. This is a foolproof way to improve your harmonic knowledge and understanding of the basic structures of popular music, as well as excellent preparation for the disciplines of composing and arranging.

At the risk of stating the obvious, each musician must listen to him or herself with the utmost attention while playing these exercises and lines, constantly striving to improve your tone production. This is the only way to reap the technical benefits of these examples. It will also lead to higher harmonic awareness, which should be complemented by analytical listening to music at all times, be it a selection to which we choose to listen at home or music heard by chance in an elevator, supermarket, or the street. To be constantly aware of musical structures, including those of styles that we dislike, is an excellent discipline. Harmonic perception can also be developed through ear training with other musicians in small groups. One person (the "player") at the piano plays cadences and harmonic sequences and the others identify first the root movements, then the quality and added tones of each chord. A more advanced level of study calls for singing each chord from bottom to top. The "player" then has to check and correct, if necessary, the notes as reproduced vocally by the other musicians. Music students at beginning levels should use the same procedure to master basic chords, starting with root position triads and seventh chords without added tones, as well as simple intervals, before attempting to identify cadences and sequences. When practicing alone, try to sing the root of each chord as you play it on your instrument. To conclude, two anecdotes:

Charlie Parker, undisputed king of the alto sax and of Bebop, was walking by a club where a country music band was playing. Country music was anathema to the beboppers, who considered it "square" compared to the subtleties of modern jazz harmony. To the astonishment of his companion, a young musician who, like all other young jazz musicians, idolized "Bird", Parker stopped at the entrance of the club and began to listen attentively to the band. When the young man complained about having to listen to that "inferior" music, Bird replied, "We always have something to learn by listening to another musician".

When my teacher, Charlie Banacos, was in the hospital in the final stage of cancer, he sent a message to his friends and students through his daughter - "Most of the electronic sounds in this hospital are B's D#'s, F#'s and A naturals... So you could say right at this moment I am swimming around in a pool of Bdom7. So you could use that as a basis, the next time you hear somebody yell "code", you can practice and name its function against the B7 chord as quickly as possible, and it makes a type of symphony... I hope you never have to use this kind of exercise in this type of situation..."

SOME THOUGHTS ON TONALITY

"The evolution of harmony is the evolution of human consciousness"
Nadia Boulanger

In Western European Classical Music, the dominant seventh chord could only be used as a dominant chord - either as a principal dominant - the fifth degree of a tonality, or as a secondary dominant - V of V, V of II, and so forth. In 1839, Frederic Chopin used a dominant seventh chord as the final tonic chord of his Prelude in F Major. Although the chord is arpeggiated, the E flat added to the F major triad is sustained with the pedal, clearly defining an F7. In the first decade of the 20th century, Alexander Scriabin began to use altered dominant seventh chords systematically as the final tonic chord of many of his piano works. At the same time, many composers such as Charles Ives, Stravinsky, Debussy, and Ravel began to free the dominant seventh from obligatory resolution, and Ives and Stravinsky introduced polytonality - two or more simultaneous key centers, further shaking the foundations of Classical Music Theory. The French composer Darius Milhaud created a wonderful synthesis of polytonality with Brazilian "ginga" (popular music time feels) in his suite for piano - "Saudades do Brasil". Arnold Schonberg introduced his 12-tone theory of music in 1923 based on tone rows drawn from the complete chromatic scale, (although he was proceeded by Bela Bartok in 1908 with his Bagatelle #3) - providing an alternative model to the Dominant - Tonic relationship which had previously dominated Western European "classical" music (the word "classical", like the word "contemporary", mean very different things to different people in different places and time frames). Schonberg's system - known as dodecaphonic or serial music, was a guiding principle for a large portion of the concert music of the 20th century, although it had little or no influence on popular music and influenced only a small number of jazz composers.

In Jazz, Blues, and other styles of popular music, the dominant seventh chord is used on an equal footing with major seventh and minor sevenths as a tonic chord. Indeed, the Blues tonality is almost exclusively based on the dominant seventh as tonic, sub-dominant, and dominant chords. The Blues Scale (1 - b3 - 3 - 4 - #4 - 5 - b7) defines a dominant seventh tonic area. Together with the Flamenco scale (1 - b2 - b3 - 3 - 4 - 5 - b6 - b7), also known as Spanish Phrygian Mode or Andalou scale (in North Africa, where it originated), the Blues Scale suggests a tonality that is neither major nor minor (or both!). These two scales have become the bedrock of many styles of popular music, none of which readily analyzable with the tools of traditional Classical Music Theory. Even further away from the traditional tonal model are the music of numerous cultures based on pentatonic scales from Africa, Asia, and native North and South American cultures, as well as Indian Classical Music, based on ragas, scales with quarter tones and thirds of a tone played over a drone or pedal point. Harmony was not an integral part of these musical styles until the 20th century, when the pervasive influences of Western European classical and United States popular music added harmonic elements (with varying degrees of esthetic success). Much of the music of Brazil's Northeast is based on modes with the dominant seventh ("minor seventh", as it is called in traditional Classical Music Theory) and mixtures of major and minor thirds in a common tonic area. A famous example in Brazilian piano music is the main theme from Camargo Guarnieri's "Dança Negra". Many sambas de enredo (themes from the Rio carnaval parades) share this major-minor ambiguity.

We may thus conclude that the traditional tools of Classical Music Harmony, including the strict segregation of major and minor keys and the absolute hegemony of the major scale and natural, melodic, and harmonic minor scales which serves as the basis for scale-degree-based analysis, are of limited relevance not only to Modern Popular Music, but to Contemporary Classical or "Art" music (the eurocentricity of these terms is sadly obvious). The 20th century composers cited above, along with Edgar Varese, Olivier Messiaen, Witold

Lutoslawski, Elliot Carter, and many others, introduced various models of tonal organization which are not analyzable using pre-20th century classical harmonic theory. These harmonic advances in turn influenced many of the great jazz composers and improvisers, as well as musicians from all over the world who create not only popular music but what Hermeto Pascoal calls "Universal Music" - music without boundaries which does not follow strict rules of harmony, style, or structure. Jazz and Blues, and later Rock, R&B, Funk and Rap have had a powerful influence on popular music around the world. Indeed, Jazz and Blues dominated worldwide popular music radio from the 1920's until the advent of Rock and Roll in the 1950's and 60's. Even such Brazilian music luminaries such as Pixinguinha, one of the inventors of the "Chorinho" style, worked originally in a Jazz band format (with a very different time feel!), as did Custodio Mesquita, a prime inspiration for Tom Jobim (who was in turn accused of being a "jazzista"). Jazz was a factor in the evolution of popular music in Africa, Asia, Latin America, and the Caribbean. And of course, this has always been a circular flow of musical cross-pollination, essential to the continuing evolution of popular music. Brasil, for example, changed popular music forever with the explosion of Bossa Nova in the 1960's.

With all this in mind, we must re-examine the notions of tonic and tonality to enable us to analyze fully and clearly Modern Popular Music. As a starting point for an honest examination of the harmonic structures of this music, let us start with a few basic principles:

1. The tonic chord may be of any quality, including any quality triad, dominant seventh, minor seventh, minor--major seventh, sus4 dominant seventh, minor-major seventh flat five, slash chords (triads with non-diatonic bass tones), and polytonal chords.

2. Each mode, including symmetrical scales such as whole town augmented, and diminished, defines its own tonality or tonal center. For example, D Dorian, E Phrygian, F Lydian, G Mixolydian, A Aeolian, and B Locrian each define their own tonic area and do not necessarily have anything to do with the theoretical "mother scale" of C Major (C Ionian). Indeed, more often than not, they are completely independent tonal areas. A classic example - "So What", from the Miles Davis album "Kind of Blue", contains two tonalities - D Dorian and Eb Dorian. Any attempt to analyze the D Dorian sections of this piece as the second degree of C Major or Eb Dorian as the second degree of Db Major would be futile - there are no C or Db major chords in this piece.

3. Modern Popular Music may be tonal without necessarily having a tonic. In other words - cycles, harmonic sequences, vamps, and other harmonic devices may or may not define a tonic in the traditional sense of the word.

4. Chords such as dominant sevenths, sus4, diminished sevenths and triads, and augmented triads, which were traditionally required to resolve, sometimes in order to complete a delayed resolution, are no longer necessarily suspensions of a tonic chord and can function as stand alone tonic chords. It follows that each chord may have a separate existence, without being tied to a key structure.

5. Any melody, even if diatonic, can be harmonized with chords drawn from many tonalities. Each chord illuminates the notes of the melody, either as upper structures or altered tones or as chord tones. When the sum of the chords in a piece does not add up to a key or a single scale or mode, I call this "Harmonic Collage", a term associated with mixed media works of Georges Braque, Max Ernst, Pablo Picasso, Robert Rauschenberg, and other 20th century artists. From diverse materials is born a new formal unity.

6. The distinction between major and minor keys, with its corollary of structures based on a hierarchy of scale degrees, is no longer omnipresent or necessary. It is useful to know the diatonic degrees of the traditional minor and major scales to analyze, for instance, the musical comedies of Broadway and much of the core repertoire of North American, South American, and European popular songs. However, composers such as Wayne Shorter, Bill Evans, Claus Ogerman, Hermeto Pascoal, Herbie Hancock, Joe Zawinul, Guinga, Chris Potter, Don Ellis, Gonzalo Rubalcaba, Maria Schneider, and Vince Mendoza have proved beyond a shadow of a doubt that it is possible to compose music that is rich in all elements of harmony, melody, and swing without the rigid structural obligations of pre-20th century Western European Classical Music or the daunting intellectuality of much of post-Schonbergian Contemporary Classical concert music.

II-7 V7/ IMaj7 CADENCES

In Guide Tones descending by whole steps. 3 and 7 enable us to hear the quality of a seventh chord with just 2 notes plus the root. An exception is m7b5, for which we need the b5 as well to define it.

In Guide Tones descending by half steps

3 Notes in the Right Hand

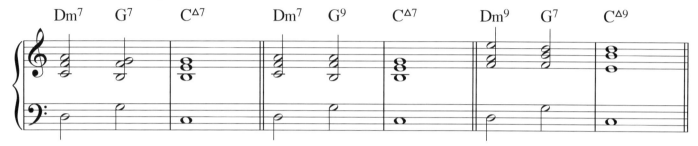

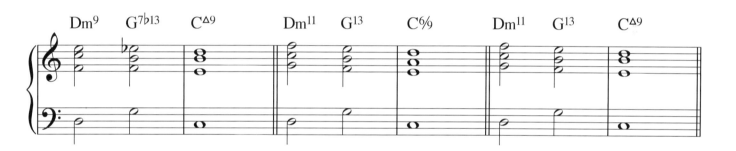

Modification of the Tonic Chord

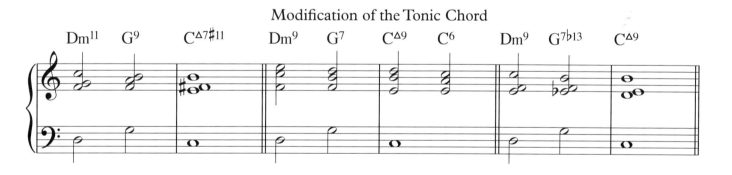

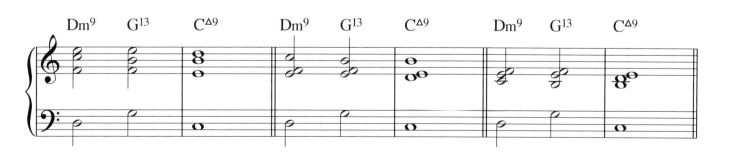

4 Notes in the Right Hand. These and other cadences should be played in all keys. Analyze the function of each note in chord to facilitate transposition.

II-7 V7/ IMaj7 CADENCES DESCENDING BY WHOLE STEPS

Start each series of cadences a half step away to learn the voicings in the other six keys

Without roots it is easier to arpeggiate these chords. Here we use Drop 2 voicings of superimposed seventh chords. Example of visualization - FMaj7/D B-7b5/G / Em7/C. See p. 126 of Volume 1

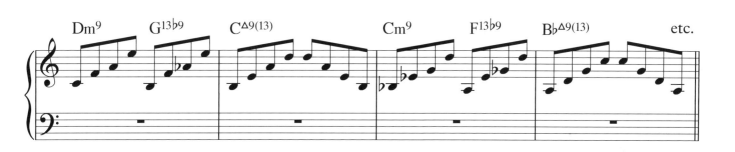

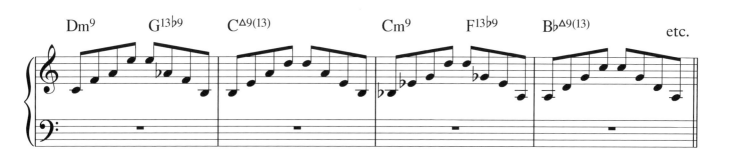

Mixed Permutations 2-1-3-4 & 3-4-2-1

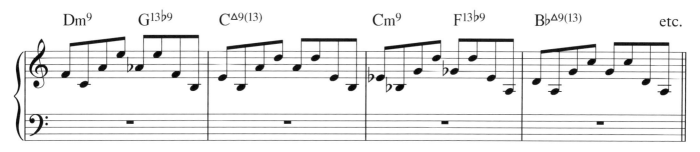

II-7 V7sus4 / IMaj7

Descending by Whole Steps

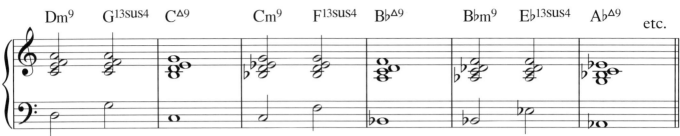
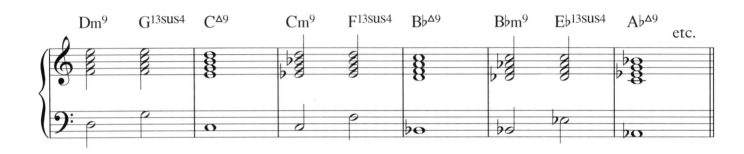
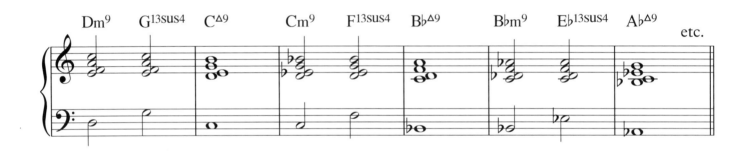
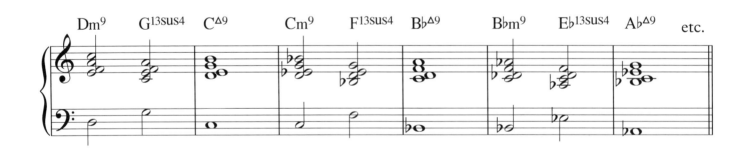
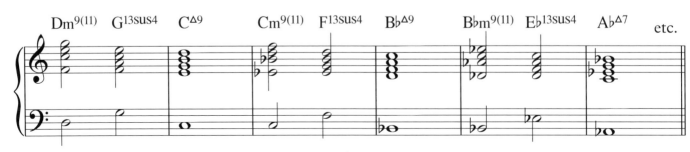

IIm7 V7 / Im7 CADENCES WITH RHYTHMIC FEELS

Apply different rhythms to II-7 V7/ IMaj7. Extend the following examples and transpose this and all series of cadences descending by whole steps a half step up to learn in all keys.

Two-Hand Positions

II V / I IN DROP 2

Major Key

See Popular Music Harmony Vol. 1 to learn how Drop 2 chords are formed

IIm7b5 V7/ Im7 CADENCES

In the chords marked * the third and/or the seventh is missing but they fit the chord symbol

bVI7 V7 / Im7 CADENCES

This cadence is formed by tritone substitution on the II degree

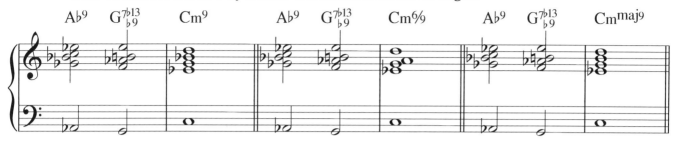

Substitution by division - insert a m7 or m7b5 a perfect fourth below VIb7 and V7

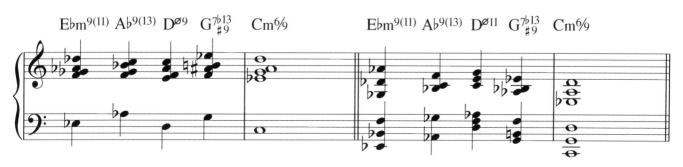

IIm7 bIIMaj7 / Im7 CADENCES

IIm7 bIIMaj7 / IMaj7 & II7 bII7 / IMaj7 CADENCES

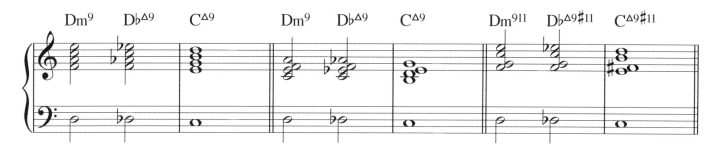

Harmonic Sequences with IIm7 bIIMaj7

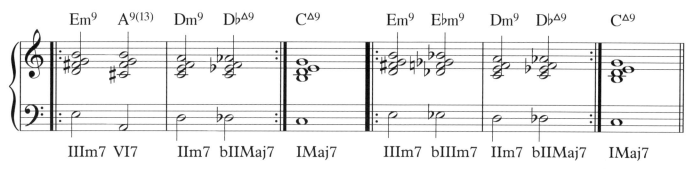

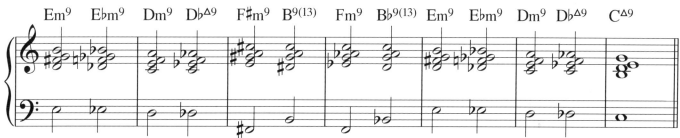

Substitution by Division - "Satin Doll"

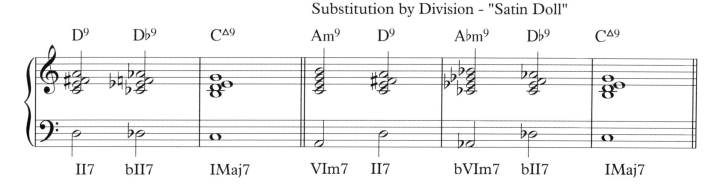

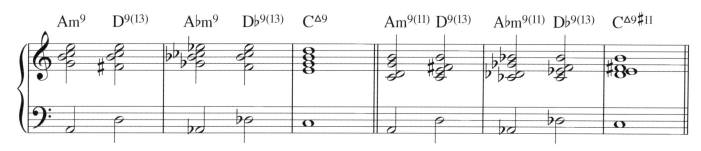

IIm7b5 V7 / Im7 CADENCES WITH RHYTHMIC FEELS

Baião - IIm7b5 V7/ Im7 descending by whole steps - 4 bars - Modification of the Tonic

II-7 V7/ I-7 - 4 notes in the right hand

IIm7 V7/ Im7 - Two Hand Voicings

MELODIC CADENCES II-7 V7 / IMAJ7

Practice each cadence descending by whole steps

II-7 V7/ Imaj7 I6 Cadences descending by half steps

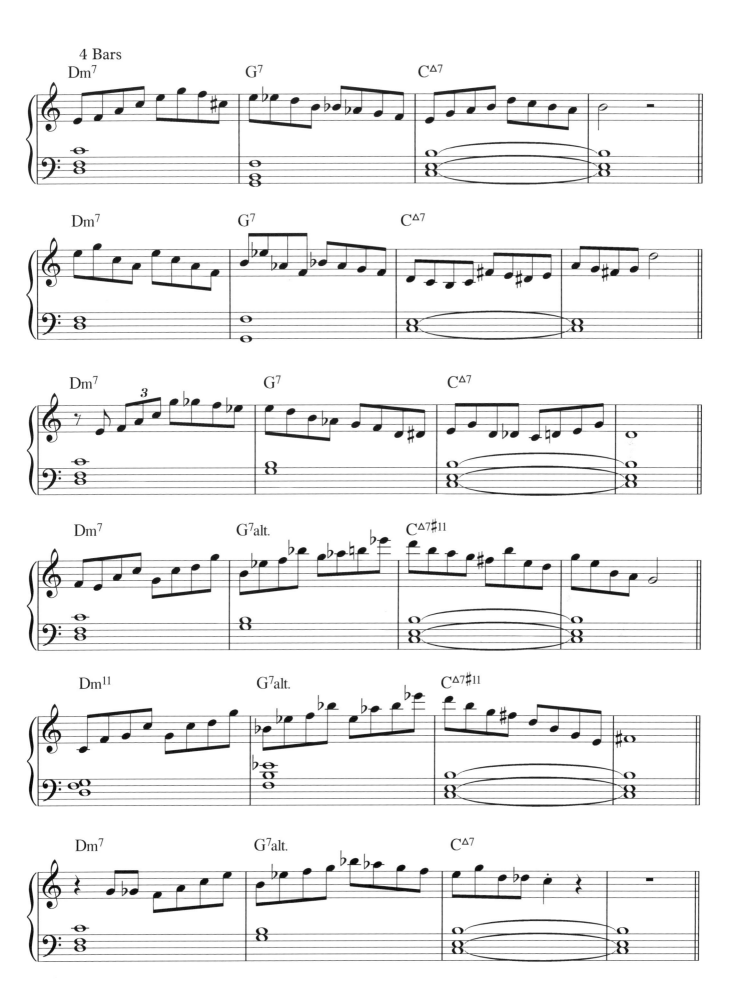

MELODIC LINE ON THE HARMONY OF "TUNE UP"

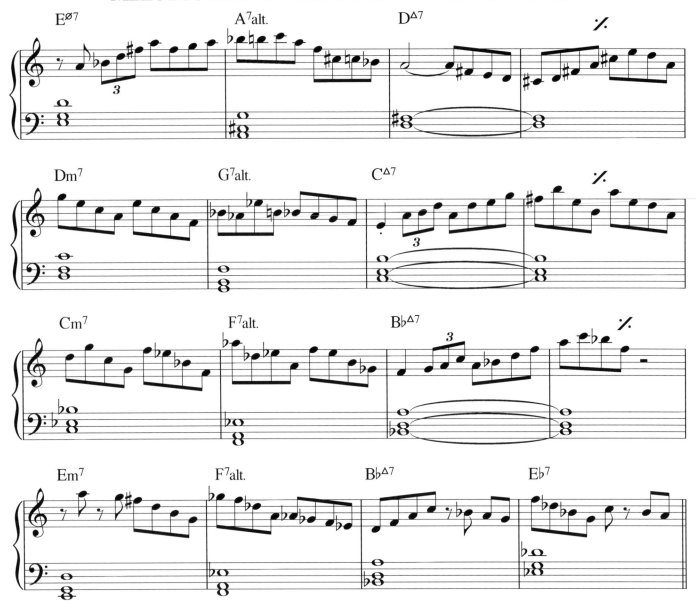

This melodic line based on the changes of "Tune Up", by Miles Davis, is an example of a composition based primarily on a series of II-7 V7/Imaj7's descending by whole steps. The line is made up mostly of superimposed seventh chords, for example, BbMaj7#5 over E, forming an Em7b5, in the first bar, an Am7 and Fmaj7 over D, outlining a Dm11 in the fifth bar, the Gmaj7 over E forming an Em9 in bar 13, an Dm7 over Bb, forming a Bbmaj9 chord in bar 19, and the Gm7b5 over Eb forming an Eb9 the final bar. Please see Popular Music Harmony Vol. 1 for a complete explanation of visualizing superimposed seventh chords. The line is filled out with fragments of chord scales corresponding to these chords, for example the G super locrian (G altered scale) in bar 6, and as well as chromatic and diatonic ornaments, known as "approach tones". These notes, present in the melodic cadences on the previous page, are explained in the following section.

APPROACH TONES

Notes may be added to arpeggiated chords. They may be diatonic (from chord scales), or chromatic. Play in all keys. Modify these examples for other chord types (ex. b5 for P5 and m6 for M6 on m7b5).

G9#11 - Passing tones in G Lydian b7

G79#11 - Diatonic from above - Chromatic from below - with doubled chord tones

Chromatic from below - Double Chromatic from above

The following exercises may be played in C ionian by substituting F for F# in the diatonic approaches

CMaj7#11 - Passing Tones in C Lydian

CMaj7#11 - Diatonic from above - Diatonic from below with doubled chord tones

CMaj7#11 - Diatonic from above - Chromatic from below with doubled chord tones

Chromatic from below - Double Chromatic from above

MELODIC LINE ON THE HARMONY OF "SOLAR"

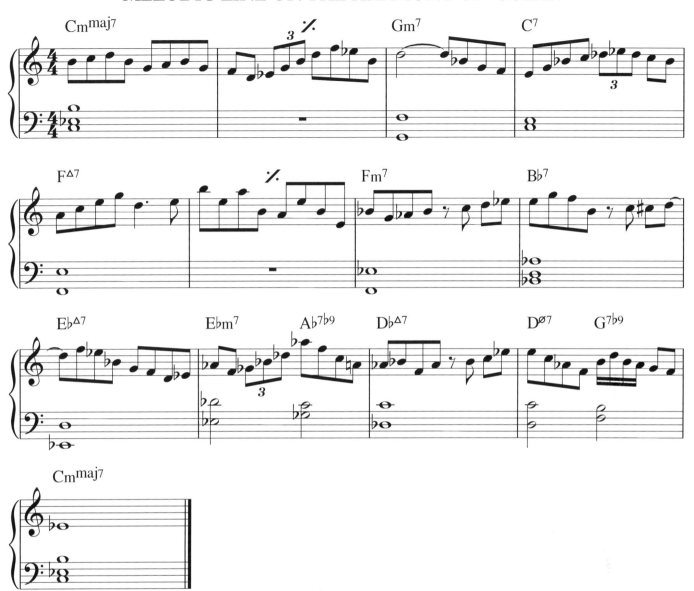

This tune by Miles Davis is an interesting harmonic structure including a combination of major and minor II V/ I cadences. Note that the harmonic rhythm, the speed at which the chords change, accelerates from the beginning to the end of the form. That is, the cadences become shorter and shorter. Also notice that the first cadence, which resolves to FMaj 7, in bars 3 to 6, establishes a major fourth degree, non-diatonic to the key of C minor. There follow two II V/ I cadences in major keys, descending by whole steps, before the final cadence: IIm7b5 V7/ImiMaj7 resolving to the tonic of C minor (mode of C melodic minor, one half step below the preceding tonal center of DbMaj7. This cadence links the last bar to the first bar of the form.

CADENCES WITH DELAYED RESOLUTION

MINOR KEY MELODIC II V/ I CADENCES

MELODIC LINE ON THE HARMONY OF "BEAUTIFUL LOVE"

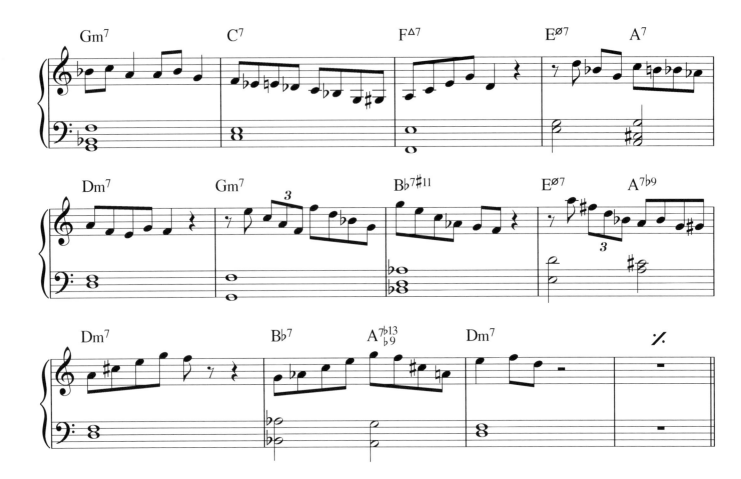

This tune, by Victor Young, starts with a II V / I cadence in D minor, followed by another in the relative major key of F. The cadence in D minor reoccurs several times, over 2 bars and 4 bars. This cadence is transformed by a substitution - Bb7 replacing Em7b5, creating a bVI7 V7 / Im7 cadence. This is an example of tritone substitution on the second scale degree.

MELODIC LINE ON THE HARMONY OF "HOW HIGH THE MOON"

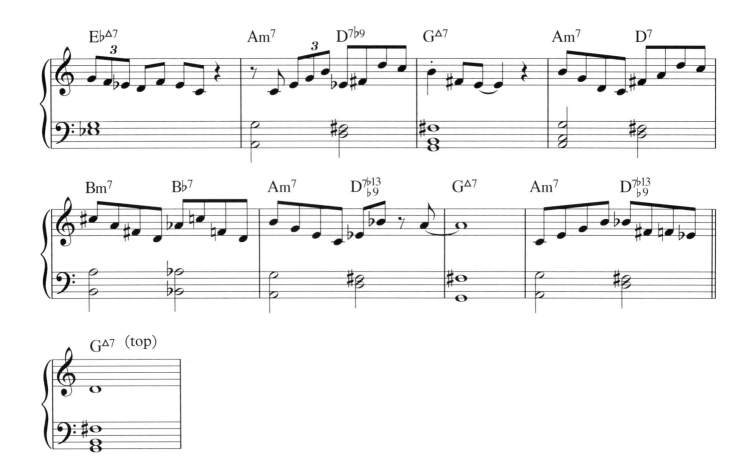

This tune, by Morgan Lewis, served as the basis for the Bop standard "Ornithology". It is an excellent example of II V / I cadences mixed with harmonic sequences. The first nine bars are built on three II-7 V7/ IMaj7 descending by whole steps. In the following section the II V motion in the bass returns three times - the first resolving to a minor tonic (Gm7), the second to a major tonic (GMaj7), and the third leading into a IIIm7 bIII7 / IIm7 V7 harmonic sequence, with the Bb7 chord functioning as a tritone substitution for the modified 6th degree - E7. The second half of the tune repeats almost all of the changes of the first half to complete the A-B-A-C form.

Try practicing melodic IIm7 V7 / I Maj7's descending by whole steps.
For example - the last two phrases of the preceding line.

CADENCES WITH A DOMINANT SEVENTH TONIC
II7 V7 / I7

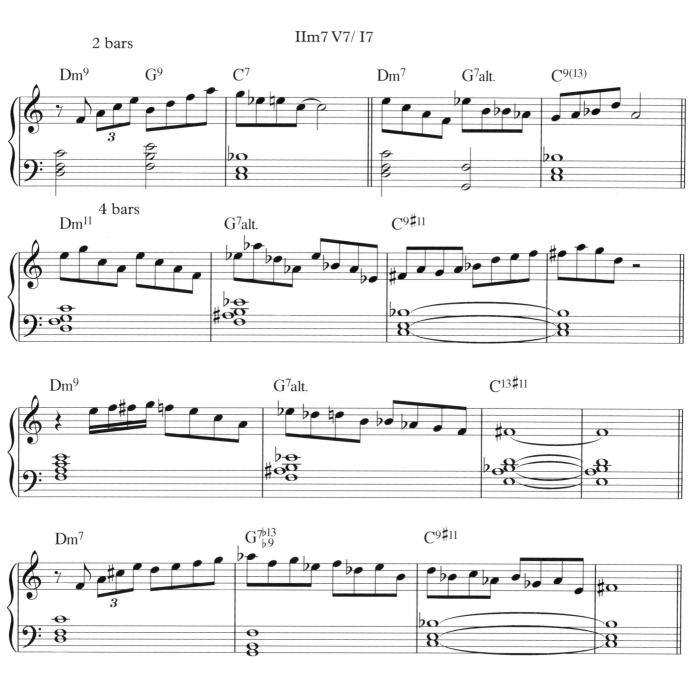

MELODIC LINE ON THE HARMONY OF "LAURA"

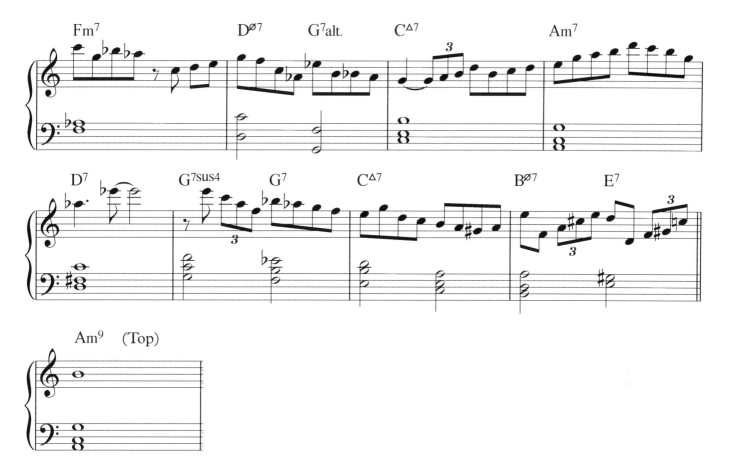

This tune, by David Raskin, begins with a series of IIm7 V7 / IMaj7 cadences descending by whole steps. This series of cadences starts again in bar 17, to be interrupted by a IIm7b5 V7 / IMaj7 cadence on the C major tonic in bars 26 and 27. The key of C is reinforced with an harmonic sequence - IMaj7 VIm7 / II7 V7, between bars 27 and 31. Completing the form, a IIm7b5 V7 / Im7 cadence which brings us back to the Ami7 (relative minor of C) in the first bar. This line contains various pentatonic scale fragments which fit the modes corresponding to the chords. For example, in bar 20, fragments of A pentatonic scale suggest the G lydian mode. In bars 23 and 24, fragments of C and G pentatonic scales are mixed to suggest F lydian.

MELODIC LINE ON THE HARMONY OF "A FOGGY DAY"

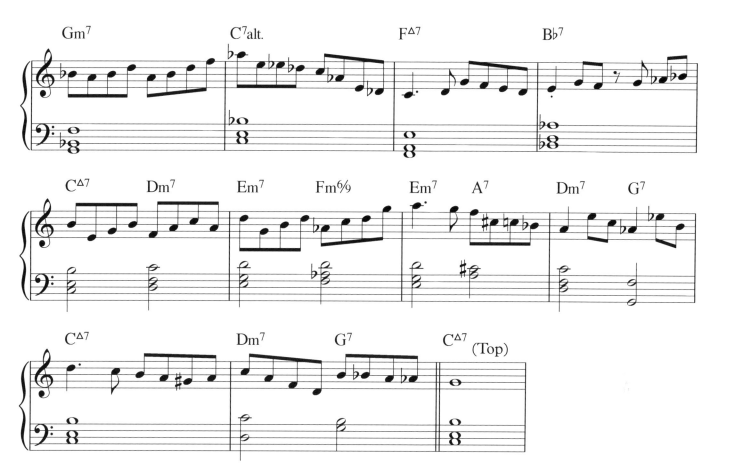

This George and Ira Gershwin evergreen begins with a IMaj7 VI7 / II7 V7 harmonic sequence which is repeated in bars 5 - 8. Each sequence is modified or "enriched" with a IIm7 V7 / I cadence on the second and fifth degrees, respectively. The same sequence, slightly modified, returns in bars 13 - 16. In the following four bars, the sequence returns, with the substitution of Ebm7 Ab7 for A7, that is, bIIIm7 bVI7 replacing VI7. In bars 29 and 30, a diatonic harmonic sequence - I IIm7 / IIIm7 IVm6 (with the fourth degree modified) leads up to a IIIm7 VI7 / IIm7 V7 harmonic sequence before resolving to the final tonic.

CHORD CHANGES FOR "A FOGGY DAY"

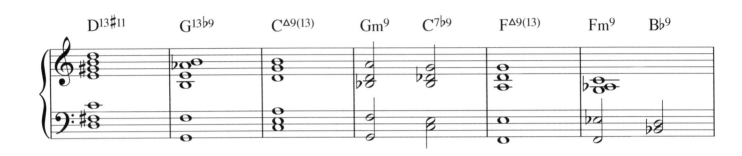
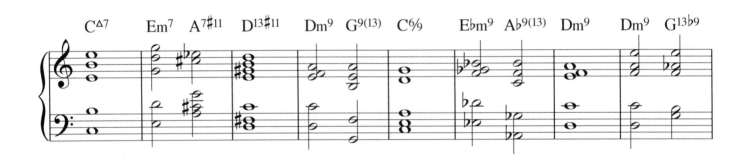
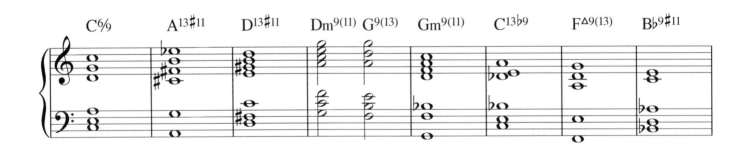
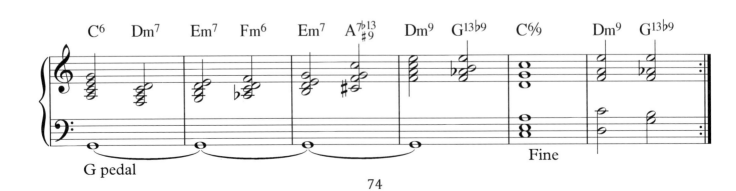

DECEPTIVE CADENCES

A deceptive cadence ends with a chord other than the tonic, usually with the tonic in the upper voice

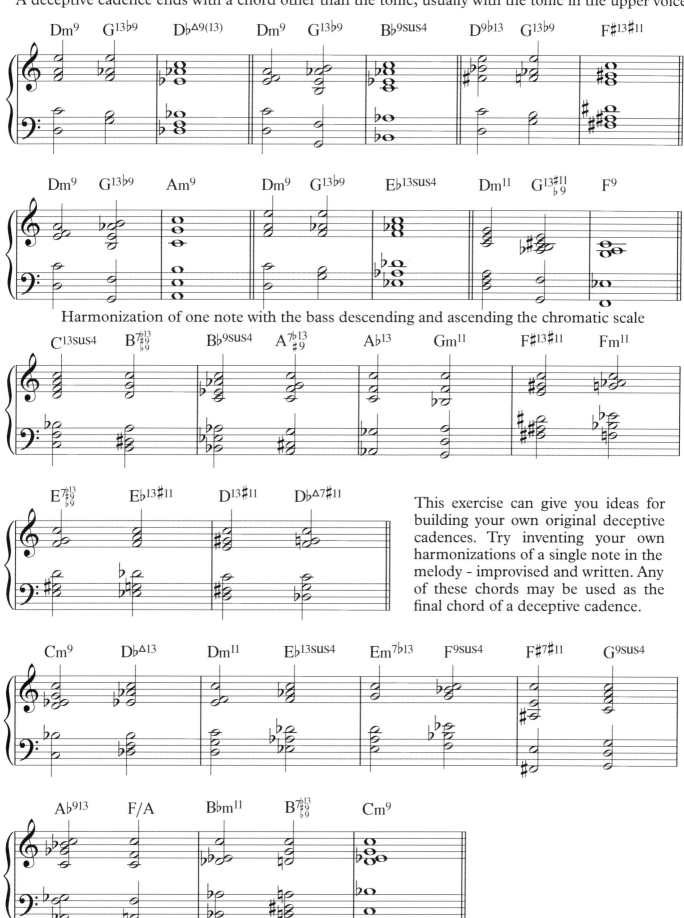

Harmonization of one note with the bass descending and ascending the chromatic scale

This exercise can give you ideas for building your own original deceptive cadences. Try inventing your own harmonizations of a single note in the melody - improvised and written. Any of these chords may be used as the final chord of a deceptive cadence.

DECEPTIVE CADENCES WITH RESOLUTION

The deceptive cadence with resolution is widely used at the end of a piece in many styles of popular music. The "surprise chord", which often reharmonizes the tonic note in the melody, is usually not part of the original form of the piece. This chord, sometimes followed by one or more additional chords, is inserted into the form of the piece at the end of the last theme where we expect the resolution of the final cadence. It is often held with a fermata, to serve as a backdrop for an improvised cadenza. In the case of a multi-chord delayed resolution, each chord has a fermata. Notice the pedal point on the tonic in the top voice of the six chords between V and I in the last example.

CHORD CHANGES FOR "BARQUINHO"

COUNTERMELODY FOR "BARQUINHO"

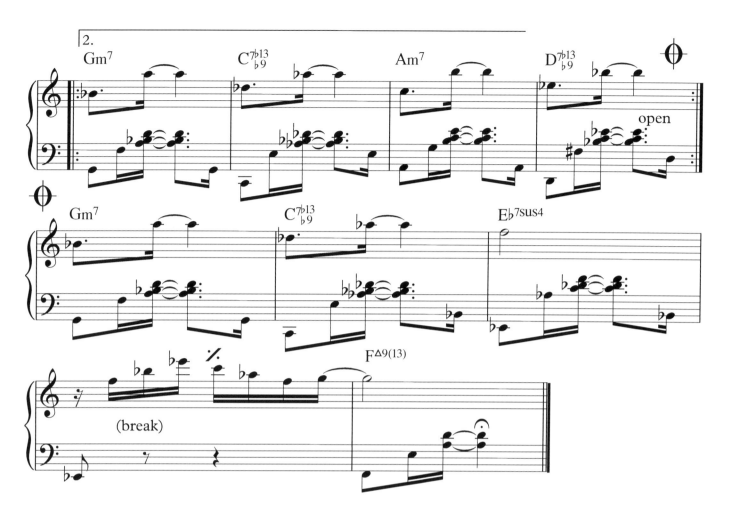

This composition by Roberto Menescal is based on a series of deceptive cadences descending by whole steps. Each cadence ends on a major seventh chord a tritone away from the expected resolution to the tonic. At the end of the form, the IIIm7 / VI7 / IIm7 / V7 harmonic sequence may also serve as an open vamp for soloing at the end of the tune. This line is a countermelody based mainly on guide tones - 3 and 7. Beginning and intermediate pianists may divide the notes in the F clef between the two hands - the left hand taking the roots and fifths, and the right hand playing the remaining notes. This arrangement includes an additional deceptive cadence in the coda - the IIm7 V7 leads to an Eb7sus4 instead of the expected tonic chord of FMaj7, then resolves to the final tonic chord (delayed resolution).

II bII/ I CADENCES

In these cadences, the fifth degree (dominant) is replaced by a chord based on bII.
This is called tritone substitution because of the interval between the two roots.

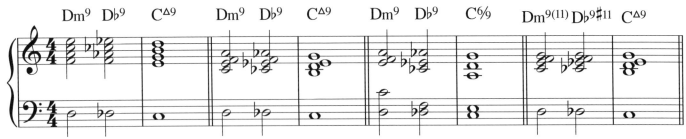

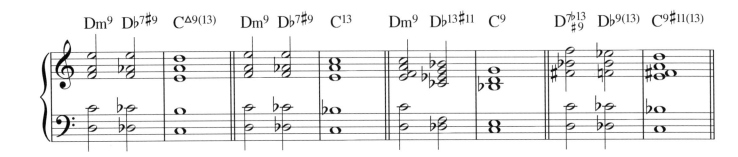

Tom Menor

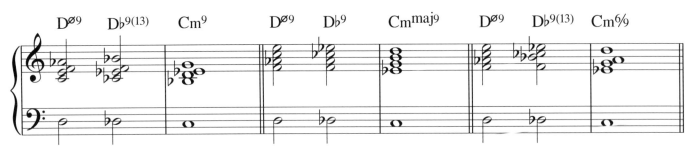

CADENCES WITH PHRYGIAN DOMINANT

The chords spelled as AbMaj7#11/G may also be called Gsus4 b9.

GOSPEL AND PLAGAL CADENCES

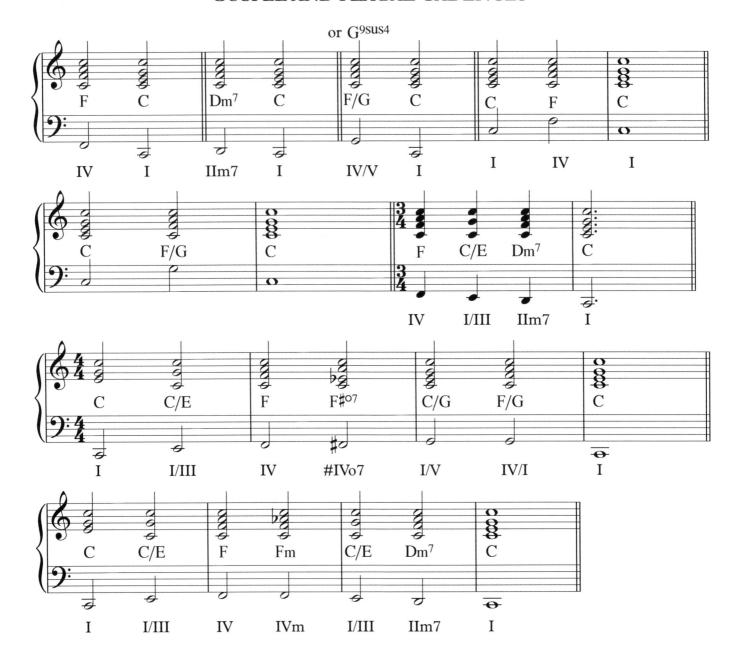

A plagal cadence resolves to the tonic from the fourth or second degree. A similar effect is produced by the resolution from a dominant seventh sus4 on the fifth degree to the tonic. This chord may also be conceived as a fourth degree major triad superimposed on the dominant. Notice that the tonic chord in gospel music is most often a triad, instead of a seventh chord, as in many other styles of popular music. This sound is also widely used in rock.

Two of these cadences use passing diminished seventh chords to enrich the harmony. The diminished seventh chord is symmetrical - made up of minor thirds which divide the octave into four equal parts, so the root may be theoretically be any one of its four tones, i.e. Cdim7 = Ebdim7 = Gbdim7 = Adim7. However, the root is commonly considered to be the semitone below the chord to which it resolves. These passing diminished chords may also be thought of as secondary dominants. In doing we may consider them as dominant seventh chords with flat nine and no root. In the example at the top of the page, F#dim7 would become D7b9, Abdim7 would become E7b9, and C#dim7 would become A7b9. This ambiguity was used extensively by Johann Sebastian Bach.

BITONAL CADENCES

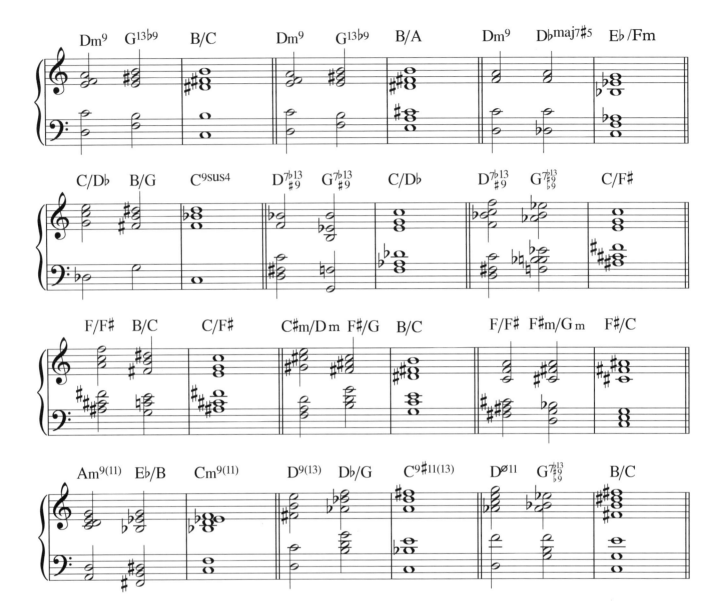

A bitonal chord contains two triadic units. A bitonal cadence may be completely or partially bitonal - that is, bitonal chords may be mixed with tonal chords, in the case of partially bitonal, or all of the chords may be bitonal, defining a fully bitonal cadence. Bitonality is a form of polytonality, or more than one simultaneous key center. A more advanced form of polytonality can use three or more simultaneous triadic units and/or key centers.

A better way to name the chords made up of two major triads would be, in the fourth measure for instance: B major triad
                                                                                        A major triad
This spelling helps to differentiate the bitonal acords from chords with a triad over a single bass note - usually called slash chords, or triads with non-diatonic bass tones. Slash chords may hint at bitonality although they do not contain two complete triads. Some bitonal chords contain a triad which corresponds to the chord traditionally used in the same place in the cadence, such as the G major triad in the next to last example. A tonal analysis of a bitonal chord is sometimes possible. For example, the last chord, B major triad over C major triad, could be called CMaj7#9#11. Bitonality is an excellent way to breathe new life into traditional harmonic structures.

CADENCES WITH Maj7#5 OR SLASH CHORDS ON V

Use these cadences to build non-traditional harmonic sequences.

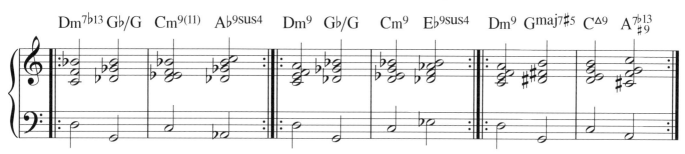

HARMONIC SEQUENCES WITH MAJOR SEVENTH TONIC

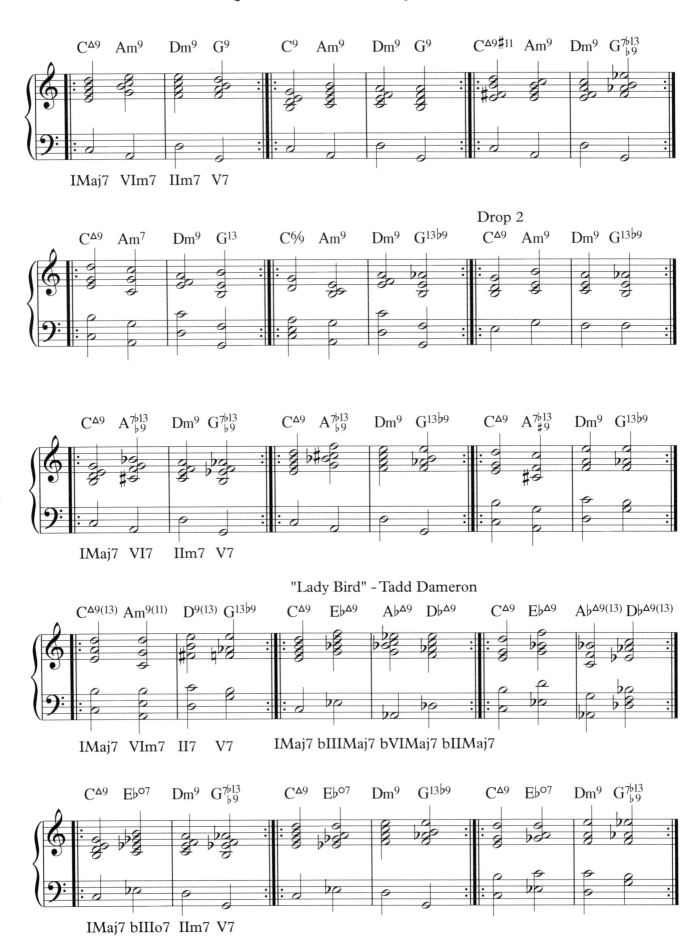

HARMONIC SEQUENCES WITH DOMINANT SEVENTH TONIC

In the following examples, the original sequence is modified by tritone substition

HARMONIC SEQUENCES WITH MINOR SEVENTH TONIC

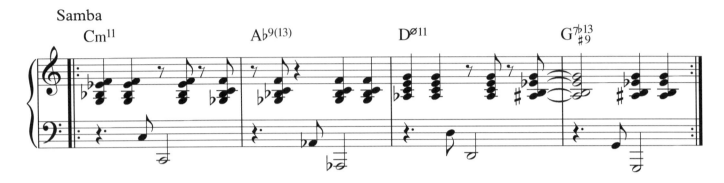

Melodic lines on this Harmonic Sequence

HARMONIC SEQUENCES STARTING ON II

Tritone substitution ★

HARMONIC SEQUENCES WITH 7SUS4 TONIC

HARMONIC SEQUENCES STARTING ON III

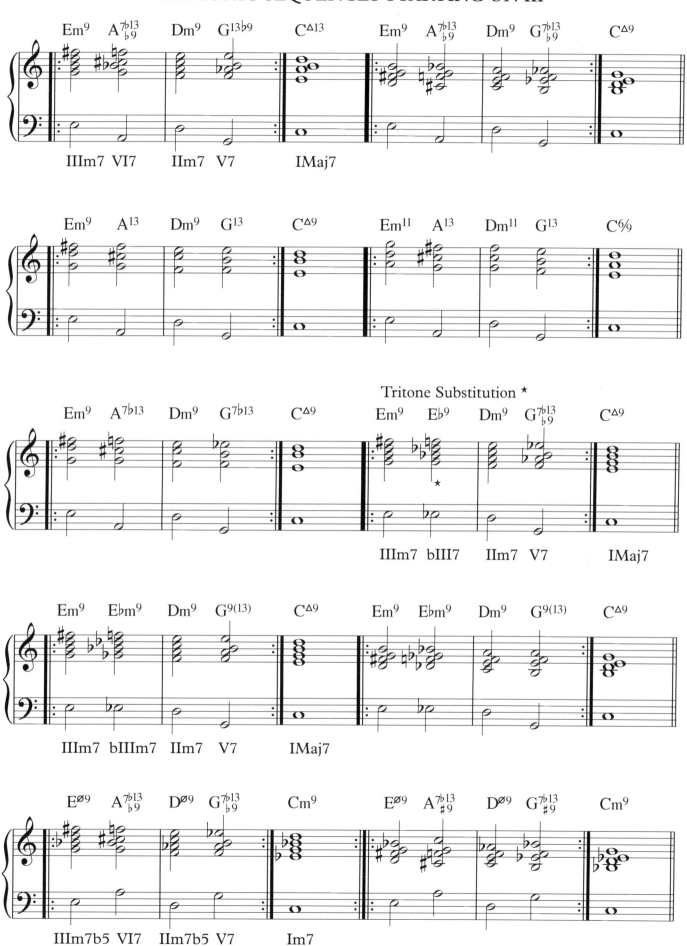

COLTRANE CHANGES

GIANT STEPS Intervallic series in the bass - m3 - P4 - m3 - P4 - m3 - P4

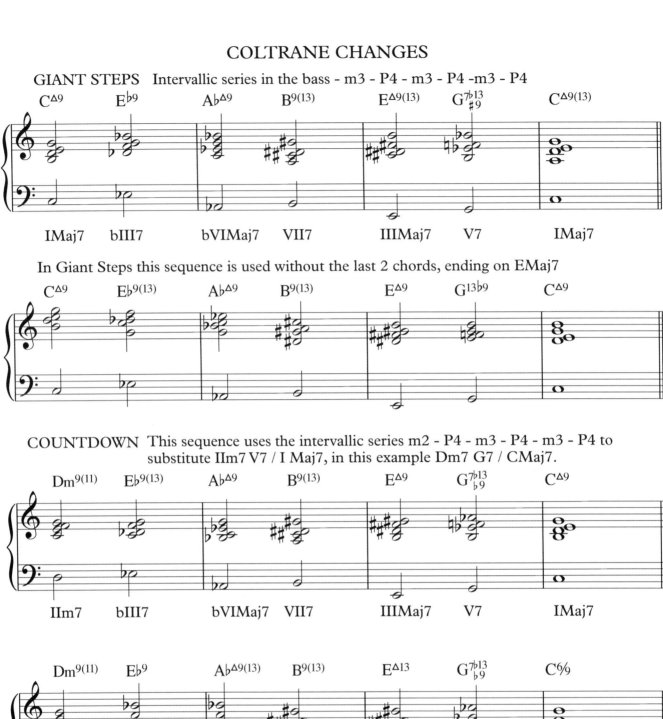

In Giant Steps this sequence is used without the last 2 chords, ending on EMaj7

COUNTDOWN This sequence uses the intervallic series m2 - P4 - m3 - P4 - m3 - P4 to substitute IIm7 V7 / I Maj7, in this example Dm7 G7 / CMaj7.

MODULATING HARMONIC SEQUENCES

Ascending by half steps

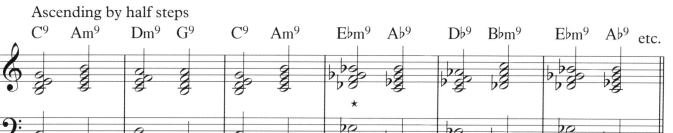

When you have mastered a harmonic sequence, you can practice it with modulation.
On the repeat ★ we raise the II V of C by a half step, transforming it into II V of Db.

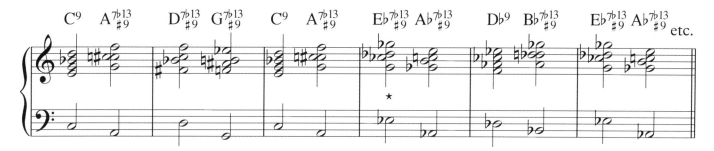

Ascending by whole steps   Raise the II V of C by a whole step ★, transforming it into II V of D.

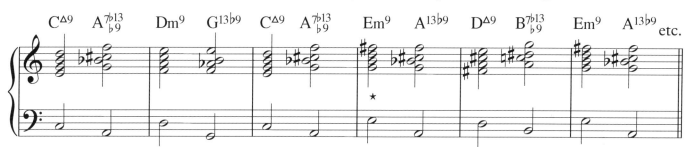

Raise the II V of D minor by a whole step ★, transforming it into II V of E minor.

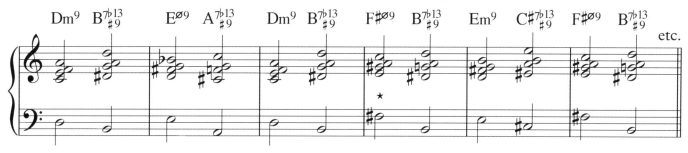

IMaj7 / VI7 / IIm7 / V7 - 4 bars

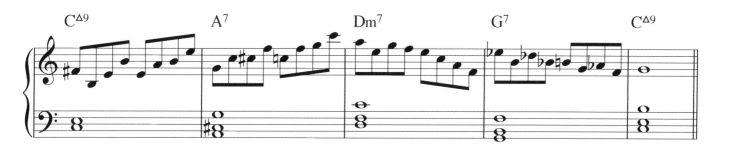

IIm7/ V7/ IMaj7/ VI7

MELODIC LINE ON THE HARMONY OF "MY ONE AND ONLY LOVE"

This tune is based on various harmonic sequences, starting with I VIm7/ IIm7 V7. The second part starts with a minor key sequence in Gm - Im7 VI-7b5/ IIm7b5 V7. Also present are several II V / I cadences, as well as fragments of the cycle of fourths/fifths with a faster harmonic rhythm in quarter notes in bars 4, 8 and 12.

Im7 VI7/ IIm7b5 V7

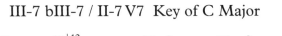

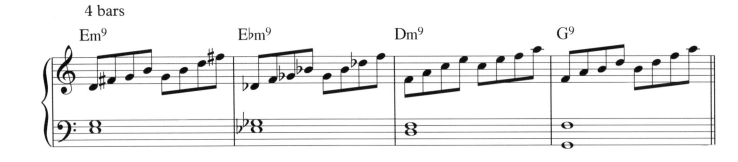

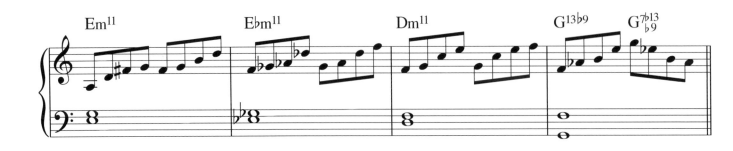

IIIm7b5 VI7 / IIm7 V7 Key of C major

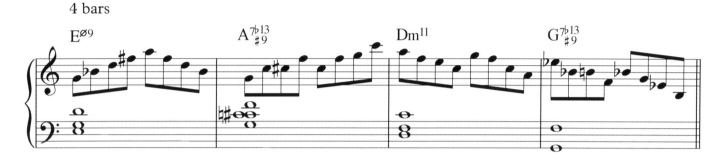

IIIm7b5 VI7 / IIm7b5 V7 Key of C minor

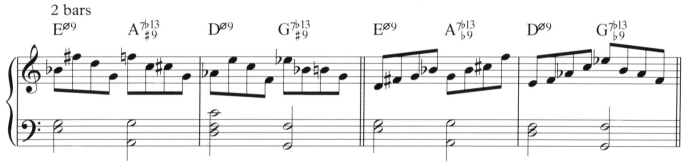

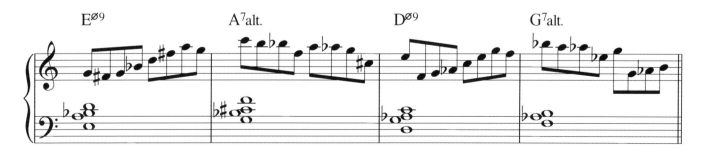

MELODIC LINE ON THE HARMONY OF "GIANT STEPS"

This tune, by John Coltrane, starts with two compound harmonic sequences - minor third ascending - perfect fourth ascending. These sequences are linked by a IIm7 V7 / IMaj7 cadence. The rest of the harmony is a series of IIm7 V7 / IMaj7 moving by major thirds, the roots forming an augmented triad. The end result leaves us in doubt as to the actual tonic chord.

Comp for "Giant Steps"

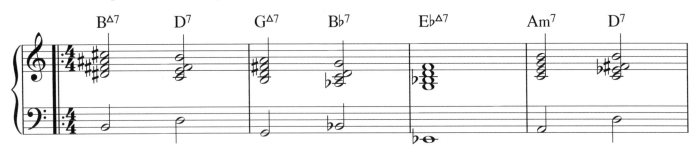

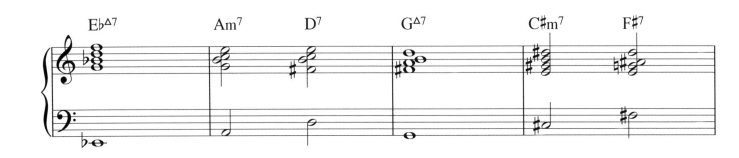
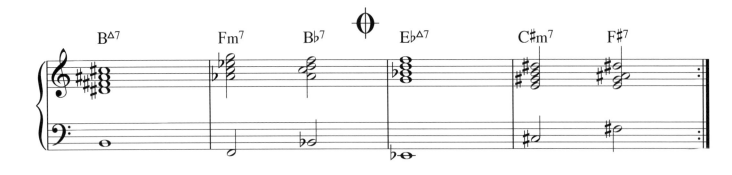

MIXED HARMONIC SEQUENCES

"Autumn Leaves"

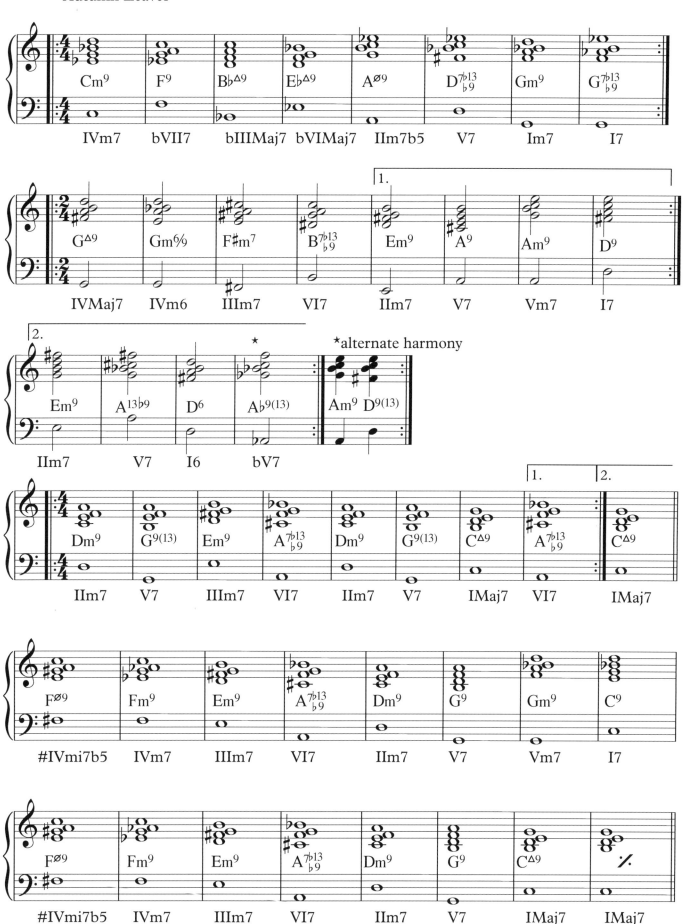

This progression combines the chromatic cycle with fragments of the cycle of fifths

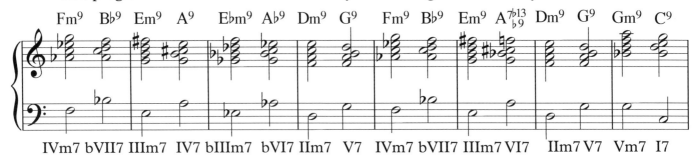

This progression mixes different harmonic sequences with fragments of the cycle of fifths

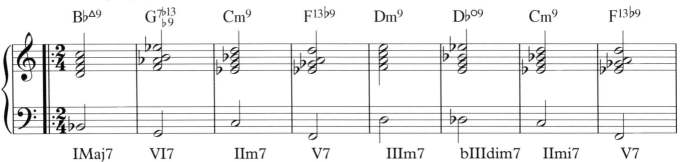

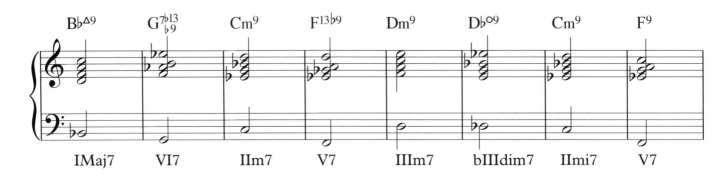

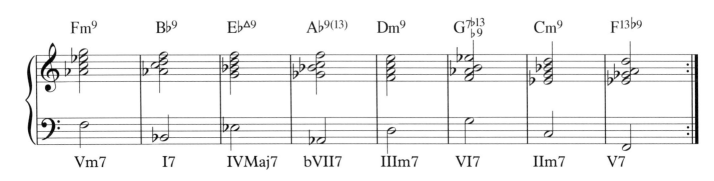

The same sequence with a melody

RHYTHM CHANGES

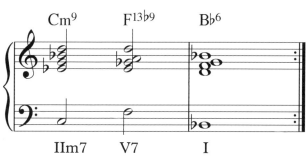

Based on "I Got Rhythm", by George Gershwin. The form is AABA. The A is based on the I VI7 / IIm7 V7 sequence, followed by fragments of the cycle of fifths. The B section follows the cycle of fifths starting on D7, an altered third degree. Note the great contrast in harmonic rhythm, four times slower at B. Musicians who play melodic instruments should practice the chords in the G clef as arpeggios.

RHYTHM CHANGES

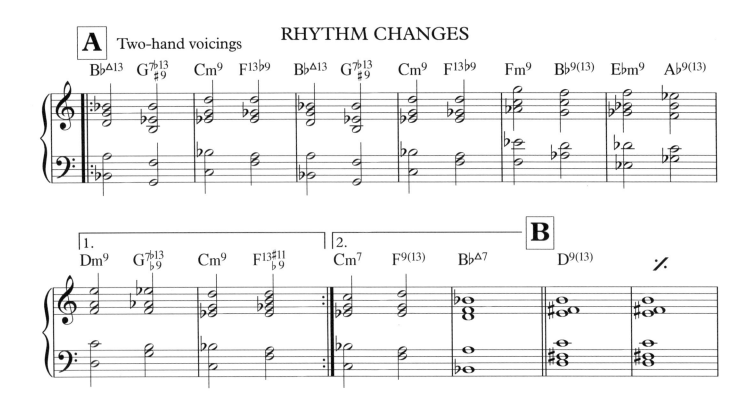
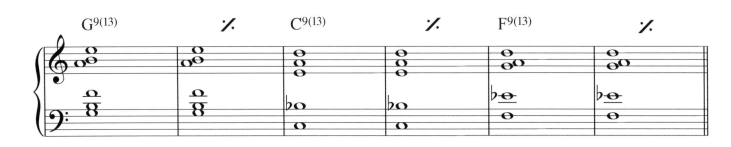

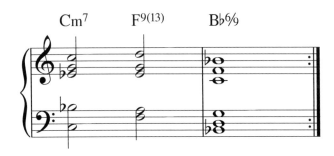

MELODIC LINE ON THE HARMONY OF "I GOT RHYTHM"

MELODIC LINE ON THE HARMONY OF "ALL OF ME"

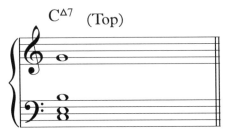

REHARMONIZATION OF "ALL OF ME"

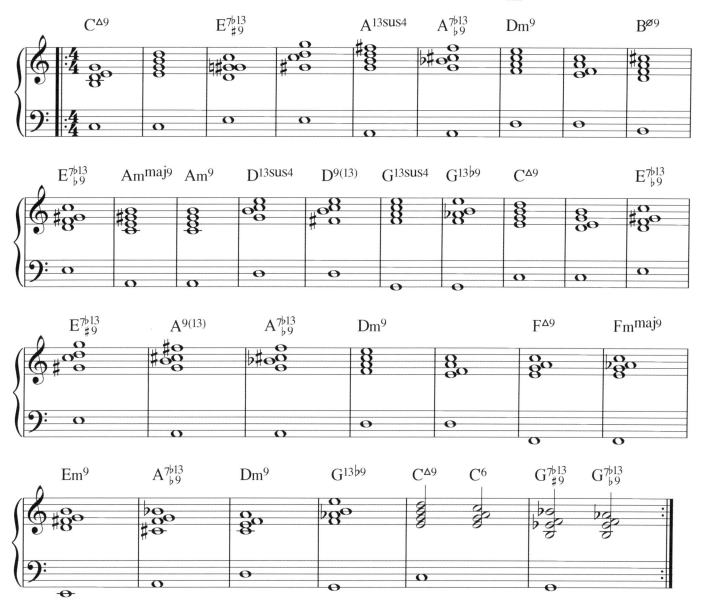

This tune uses the cycle of fifths together with cadences and harmonic sequences. When comparing this reharmonization with the basic harmony, shown in the preceding solo, notice the use of various techniques of substitution and harmonic enrichment common in popular music. These techniques include:

1. Division of two bars of a dominant seventh into one bar each of II and V of a II V / I cadence. For example, the two bars of E7 in bars 9 and 10 are transformed into one bar each of Bm7b5 and E7, forming a II V / I cadence in A minor.
2. Division of two bars of a dominant seventh into one bar each of a dominant seventh sus4 and a dominant seventh chord with the same root. For example, in bars 5 and 6, the A7 chord is divided into one bar each of A7sus4 and A7. To emphasize this transformation of the chord quality, the 13th moves to a b13th and the 9th moves to a b9, to prepare a smoother transition to Dm7. Other examples can be found in bars 13 and 14 and 15 and 16.
3. Modification of a minor chord. The Am7 chord, which lasts two bars in the original version, is divided into one bar each of AmMaj7 and Am7.
4. Modification of the alterations of a dominant seventh chord. Bars 19 and 20 and 21 and 22 demonstrate this technique. In bar 32, the two G7 chords create an interesting movement in the upper voice through the transformation of #9 into b9.

The aim of these harmonic modifications is to create an accompaniment with an interesting counter line in the upper voice of the chords and to facilitate smooth voice leading.

HARMONIC SEQUENCES WITH PEDAL POINTS

II / V / I / VI

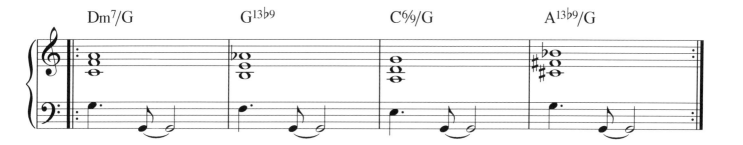

In a minor key we can mix m7, mMaj7 and m6/9 as the tonic

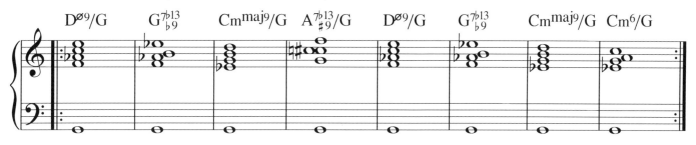

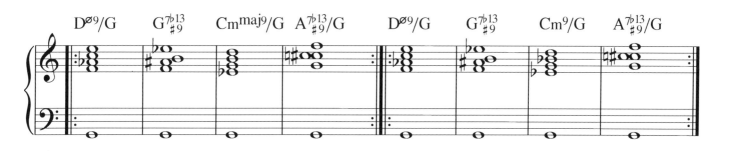

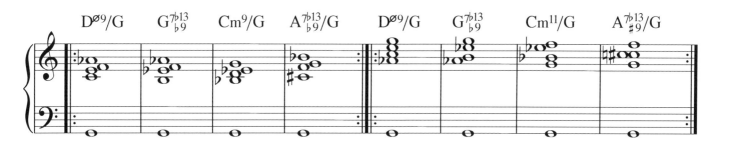

Drop 2

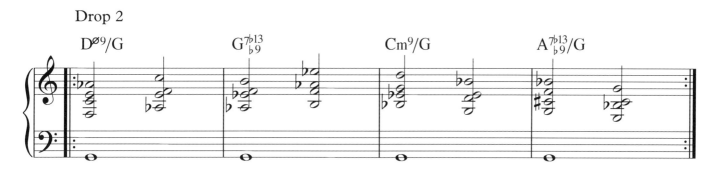

IMaj7 VI7 / IIm7 V7

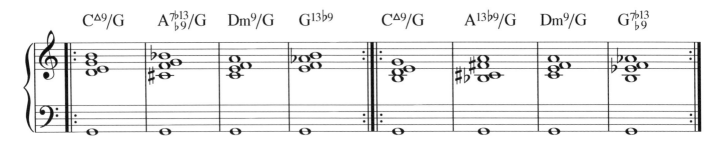

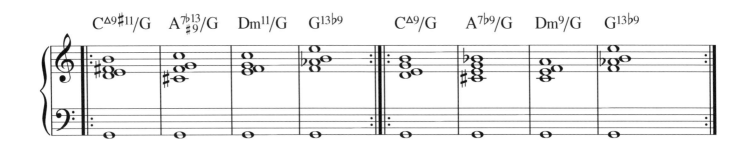

IMaj7 VIm7 / IIm7 V7

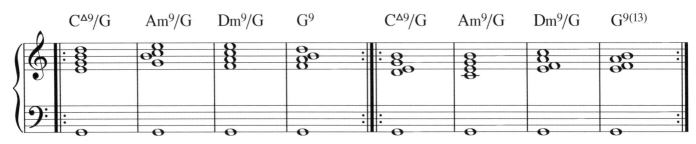

Drop 2

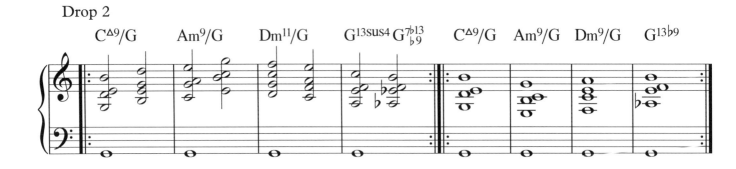

In a major key we can mix VIm7 and VI7

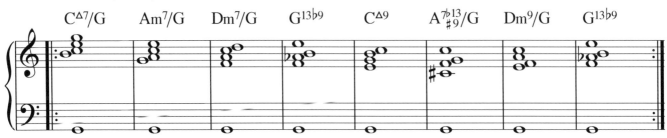

"SOMEDAY MY PRINCE WILL COME" WITH PEDAL POINT
Comp for the Miles Davis version with a dominant pedal point on the entire form

COMPOSITION EXERCISES
WITH CADENCES AND HARMONIC SEQUENCES

1. Write a composition using at least 3 II V / I cadences descending by whole steps mixed with cycle of fifths root movements.

2. Write a composition using major and minor cadences, varying the intervals between the tonics.

3. Write a composition using at least 3 II V / I cadences each in minor and major keys.

4. Write a composition using at least 4 II V / I cadences mixed with harmonic sequences.

5. Write a composition mixing a blues form with harmonic sequences.

6. Write a composition using only minor key II V / I's.

7. Write a composition using only major key II V / I's.

8. Write a composition using II V / I cadences modified by division in pairs

of m7 and dom7. Modal borrowing may be used.

9. Write a composition using minor harmonic sequences linked with 4 and/or 8 bar modal sections.

10. Write a composition using harmonic sequences modulating up and/or down by whole steps and half steps. Link the sequences with cycle of fifths root movements.

11. Write a melodic line on the changes of each standard in this book.

12. Write a harmonic line on the A section of "I Got Rhythm" with a B section using II V / I cadences moving by minor thirds.

13. Write a composition using Gospel cadences.

14. Write a composition using at least 3 harmonic sequences over pedal points on the dominant, mixed with II V / I cadences.

MUSIC FOR ANALYSIS

1. Anthropology - Dizzy Gillespie & Charlie Parker

2. Jump Monk - Charles Mingus

3. Desafinado - Tom Jobim & Newton Mendonça

4. Cherokee - Ray Noble

5. I Can't Get Started - Vernon Duke

6. Peace - Horace Silver

7. You Are Too Beautiful - Richard Rogers & Lorenz Hart

8. Turn Out the Stars - Bill Evans

9. Pensativa - Clare Fischer

10. Começar de Novo (The Island) - Ivan Lins

11. Corsario - João Bosco

12. Seu Chopin Desculpe - Johnny Alf

13. Four - Miles Davis

14. Beijo Partido - Toninho Horta

15. Senhorinha - Guinga

16. Lush Life - Billy Strayhorn

17. Minha - Francis Hime

18. Velho Piano - Dori Caymmi

19. Lady Bird - Tadd Dameron

20. Round Midnight - Thelonious Monk

Also available:

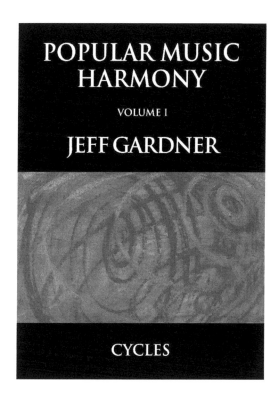

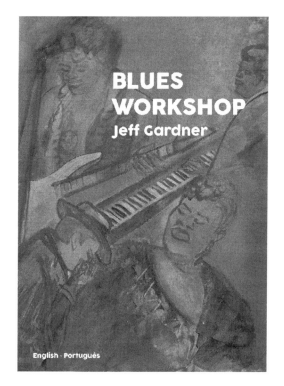
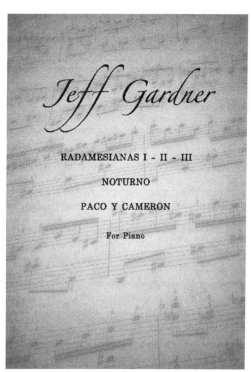

For purchase information please visit
www.jeffgardner.com.br

Copyright @ 2016 by Jeff Gardner.

Printed in Poland
by Amazon Fulfillment
Poland Sp. z o.o., Wrocław